CRITICAL MISCELLANIES

Vol.- III

Essay 5: On Pattison's Memoirs

by

John Morley

CRITICAL MISCELLANIES
Vol.- III
Essay 5: On Pattison's Memoirs
by John Morley

Copyright © 2023

ISBN: 978-93-60467-41-8

Published by

DOUBLE 9 BOOKS

2/13-B, Ansari Road
Daryaganj, New Delhi – 110002
info@double9books.com
www.double9books.com
Tel. 011-40042856

ABOUT THE AUTHOR

JOHN MORLEY Born on December 24, 1838, John Morley was the 1st Viscount Morley of Blackburn, OM, PC, FRS, FBA. He died on September 23, 1923, and was a British Liberal politician, author, and newspaper editor. He started out as a reporter in the North of England and then became editor of the newly liberal Pall Mall Gazette from 1880 to 1883. In 1883, he was chosen as a Liberal Party Member of Parliament (MP). In 1886, 1892, and 1895, he was Chief Secretary for Ireland. From 1905 to 1910 and again in 1911, he was Secretary of State for India. From 1910 to 1914, he was Lord President of the Council. Morley was a well-known political analyst and wrote a biography of William Gladstone, who was his hero. His works and "reputation as the last of the great nineteenth-century Liberals" made Morley famous. He was against the Second Boer War and empire. He believed that Ireland should have Home Rule. He quit the government in August 1914 because he didn't want Britain to join the First World War as a Russian friend.

CONTENTS

ON PATTISON'S MEMOIRS[1]

To reckon the subject of this volume among leading minds who have stamped a deep influence on our generation, is not possible even to the friendliest partiality. That was not his position, and nobody could be less likely than he would himself have been to claim it. Pattison started no new problem. His name is associated with no fertile speculation, and with no work of the first degree of importance. Nor was he any more intended for a practical leader than for an intellectual discoverer. He did not belong to the class of authoritative men who are born to give decisions from the chair. Measured by any standard commensurate to his remarkable faculties, Pattison's life would be generally regarded as pale, negative, and ineffectual. Nevertheless, it is undeniable that he had a certain singular quality about him that made his society more interesting, more piquant, and more sapid than that of many men of a far wider importance and more commanding achievement.

[1] *Memoirs*. By Mark Pattison, late Rector of Lincoln College, Oxford. London, 1885.

Critics have spoken of his learning, but the description is only relatively accurate. Of him, in this respect, we may say, what he said of Erasmus. 'Erasmus, though justly styled by Muretus, *eruditus sane vir ac multæ lectionis*, was not a learned man in the special sense of the word—not an *érudit*. He was the man of letters. He did not make a study a part of antiquity for its own sake, but used it as an instrument of culture.' The result of culture in Pattison's actual life was not by any means ideal. For instance, he was head of a college for nearly a quarter of a century, and except as a decorative figure-head with a high literary reputation, he did little more to advance the working interests of his college during these five-and-twenty years than if he had been one of the venerable academic abuses of the worst days before reform. But his temperament, his reading, his recoil from Catholicism, combined with the strong reflective powers bestowed upon him by nature, to produce a personality that was unlike other people, and infinitely more curious and salient than many who had a firmer grasp of the art of right living. In an age of effusion to be reserved, and in days of universal professions of sympathy to show a saturnine front, was to be an original. There was nobody in whose company one felt so much of the ineffable comfort of being quite safe against an attack of platitude. There was nobody on whom one might so surely count in the course of an hour's talk for some stroke of irony or pungent suggestion, or, at the worst, some significant, admonitory, and almost luminous manifestation of the great *ars tacendi*. In spite of his copious and ordered knowledge, Pattison could hardly be said to have an affluent mind. He did not impart intellectual direction like Mill, nor morally impress himself like George Eliot. Even in pithy humour he was inferior to Bagehot, who was certainly one of the most remarkable of the secondary figures of our generation. But he made every one aware of contact with the reality of a living intelligence. It was evident that he had no designs upon you. He was not thinking of shaking a conviction, nor even of surprising admiration.

Everlasting neutrality, no doubt, may soon become a tiresome affectation. But we can afford to spare a few moments from our solid day to the Sage, if we are so lucky as to hit upon one; always provided that he be not of those whom La Bruyère has described as being made into sages by a certain natural mediocrity of mind. Whatever else may be said of Pattison, at least he was never mediocre, never vapid, trite, or common. Nor was he one of those false pretenders to the judicial mind, who 'mistake for sober sense And wise reserve, the plea of indolence.' On the contrary, his industry and spirit of laborious acquisition were his best credentials. He was invested to our young imaginations with the attraction of the literary explorer, who had 'voyaged through strange seas of thought alone,' had traversed broad continents of knowledge, had ransacked all the wisdom of printed books, and had by native courage and resource saved himself from the engulfing waters of the great Movement.

The Memoirs of such a man may not be one of the monuments of literature. His little volume is not one of those romantic histories of the soul, from the Confessions of Augustine to the Confessions of Jean Jacques, by which men and women have been beguiled, enlightened, or inspired in their pilgrimage. It is not one of those idealised and highly embellished versions of an actual existence, with which such superb artists as George Sand, Quinet, and Renan, have delighted people of good literary taste. What the Rector has done is to deliver a tolerably plain and unvarnished tale of the advance of a peculiar type of mind along a path of its own, in days of intellectual storm and stress. It stirs no depths, it gives no powerful stimulus to the desire after either knowledge or virtue—in a word, it does not belong to the literature of edification. But it is an instructive account of a curious character, and contains valuable hints for more than one important chapter in the mental history of the century.

Mark Pattison, born in 1813, passed his youthful days at the rectory of Hauxwell, a village in Wensleydale, on the edge of the great uplands that stretch northwards towards Richmond and Barnard Castle, and form an outwork of the Pennine range and the backbone of northern England. The scene has been described in that biography of his Sister Dora, which he here so unceremoniously despatches as a romance. 'Hauxwell is a tiny village lying on the southern slope of a hill, from whence an extensive view of the moors and Wensleydale is obtained. It contains between two and three hundred inhabitants. The rectory is a pretty little dwelling, some half-mile from the church, which is a fine old building much shut in by trees. The whole village, even on a bright summer day, gives the traveller an impression of intense quiet, if not of dulness; but in winter, when the snow lies thickly for weeks together in the narrow lane, the only thoroughfare of the place; when the distant moors also look cold in their garment of white, and the large expanse of sky is covered with leaden-coloured clouds; when the very streams with which the country abounds are frozen into silence—then indeed may Hauxwell be called a lonely village.'

Pattison's father had been educated, badly enough, at Brasenose, but though his own literary instincts were of the slightest, he had social ambition enough to destine his son from the first to go to Oxford and become the fellow of a college. But nothing systematic was done towards making the desired consummation a certainty or even a probability. The youth read enormously, but he did not remember a tenth of what he read, nor did he even take in the sense of half of it as he went along. 'Books as books,' he says, 'were my delight, irrespective of their contents. I was already marked out for the life of a student, yet little that was in the books I read seemed to find its way into my mind.' He found time for much besides reading. He delighted in riding, in shooting rooks in the Hall rookery, and in fishing for trout with clumsy tackle and worm. Passion for country sports was followed by passion for natural history in the ordinary shape of the boy's fancy for collecting insects and observing birds. He fell in with White's *Natural History of Selborne*, read it over and over again, and knew it by heart.

> The love of birds, moths, butterflies, led on to the love of landscape; and altogether, in the course of the next six or seven years, grew and merged in a conscious and declared poetical sentiment and a devoted reading of the poets. I don't suppose the temperament was more inclined to æsthetic emotion in me than in other youths; but I was highly nervous and delicate, and having never been at school had not had sentiment and delicacy crushed out of me; also, living on the borderland of oak woods, with green lanes before me, and an expanse of wild heather extending into Northumberland behind, I was favourably placed for imbibing a knowledge by contrast of the physical features of England. My eye was formed to take in at a glance, and to receive delight from contemplating, as a whole, a hill and valley formation. Geology did not come in till ten years later to complete the cycle of thought, and to give that intellectual foundation which is required to make the testimony of the eye, roaming over an undulating surface, fruitful and satisfying. When I came in after years to read *The Prelude* I recognised, as if it were my own history which was being told, the steps by which the love of the country-boy for his hills and moors grew into poetical susceptibility for all imaginative presentations of beauty in every direction.

Perhaps it may be added that this was a preparation for something more than merely poetical susceptibility. By substituting for the definite intellectual impressions of a systematic education, vague sensibilities as the foundation of character, this growth of sentiment, delicacy, and feeling for imaginative presentations of beauty, laid him peculiarly open to the religious influences that were awaiting him in days to come at Oxford.

In 1832 Pattison went up as a freshman to Oriel. His career as an undergraduate was externally distinguished by nothing uncommon, and promised nothing remarkable. He describes himself as shy, awkward, boorish, and mentally shapeless and inert. In 1833, however, he felt what he describes as the first stirrings of intellectual life within him. 'Hitherto I have had no mind, properly so-called, merely a boy's intelligence, receptive of anything I read or heard. I now awoke to the new idea of finding the reason of things; I began to suspect that I might have much to unlearn, as well as to learn, and that I must clear my mind of much current opinion which had lodged there. The principle of rationalism was born in me, and once born it was sure to grow, and to become the master idea of the whole process of self-education on which I was from this time forward embarked.' In other words, if he could have interpreted and classified his own intellectual type, he would have known that it was the Reflective. Reflection is a faculty that ripens slowly; the prelude of its maturity is often a dull and apparently numb-witted youth. Though Pattison conceived his ideal at the age of twenty, he was five-and-forty before he finally and deliberately embraced it and shaped his life in conformity to it. The principle of rationalism, instead of growing, seemed for twelve whole years to go under, and to be completely mastered by the antagonistic principles of authority, tradition, and transcendental faith.

The secret is to be found in what is the key to Pattison's whole existence, and of what he was more conscious at first than he seems to have been in later days. He was affected from first to last by a profound weakness of will and character. Few men of eminence have ever lived so destitute of nerve as Pattison was—of nerve for the ordinary demands of life, and of nerve for those large enterprises in literature for which by talent and attainment he was so admirably qualified. The stamp of moral *défaillance* was set upon his brow from the beginning. It was something deeper in its roots than the temporary self-consciousness of the adolescent that afflicted him in his early days at Oxford. The shy and stiff undergraduate is a familiar type enough, and Pattison is not the only youth of twenty of whom such an account as his own is true:—

> This inability to apprehend the reason of my social ill
> success had a discouraging consequence upon the growth
> of my character. I was so convinced that the fault was in me,
> and not in the others, that I lost anything like firm footing,
> and succumbed to or imitated any type, or set, with which

I was brought in contact, esteeming it better than my own, of which I was too ashamed to stand by it and assert it. Any rough, rude, self-confident fellow, who spoke out what he thought and felt, cowed me, and I yielded to him, and even assented to him, not with that yielding which gives way for peace's sate, secretly thinking itself right, but with a surrender of the convictions to his mode of thinking, as being better than my own, more like men, more like the world.

This fatal trait remained unalterable to the very end, but as time went on things grew worse. Nobody knows what deliberate impotence means who has not chanced to sit upon a committee with Pattison. Whatever the business in hand might be, you might be sure that he started with the firm conviction that you could not possibly arrive at the journey's end. It seemed as if the one great principle of his life was that the Sons of Zeruiah must be too hard for us, and that nobody but a simpleton or a fanatic would expect anything else. 'With a manner,' he says of himself, 'which I believe suggested conceit, I had really a very low estimate of myself as compared with others. I could echo what Bishop Stanley says of himself in his journal: "My greatest obstacle to success in life has been a want of confidence in myself, under a doubt whether I really was possessed of talents on a par with those around me."' Very late in life, talking to Mr. Morison, he said in his pensive way, 'Yes, let us take our worst opinion of ourselves in our most depressed mood. Extract the cube root of that, and you will be getting near the common opinion of your merits.'

He describes another side of the same over-spreading infirmity when he is explaining why it was always impossible for him ever to be anything but a Liberal. 'The restlessness of critical faculty,' he says, 'has done me good service when turned upon myself. *I have never enjoyed any self-satisfaction in anything I have, ever done,* for I have inevitably made a mental comparison with how it might have been better done. The motto of one of my diaries, "Quicquid hic operis fiat pœnitet" may be said to be the motto of my life' (p. 254). A man who enters the battle on the back of a charger that has been hamstrung in this way, is predestined to defeat. A frequent access of dejection, self-abasement, distrust, often goes with a character that is energetic, persevering, effective, and reasonably happy. To men of strenuous temper it is no paradox to say that a fit of depression is often a form of repose. It was D'Alembert, one of the busiest of the workers of a busy century, who said this, or something to this effect—that low spirits are only a particular name for the mood in which we see our aims and acts for what they really are. Pattison's case was very different. With him, except for a very few short years, despair was a system, and an unreasoned pessimism the most rooted assurance of his being. He tells a thoroughly characteristic story of himself in his days as an undergraduate. He was on the coach between Birmingham and Sheffield. Two men shared the front seat with him, and conversed during the whole of the journey about the things which he was yearning to know and to learn. 'I tried once or twice to put in my oar, but it was a failure: I was too far below their level of knowledge; I relapsed into enchanted listening. I thought to myself, "There exists then such a world, but I am shut out of it, not by the accidents of college, but by my own unfitness to enter"'. Mankind suffers much from brassy incompetency and over-complacency, but Pattison is only one of many examples how much more it may lose in a man who has ability, but no fight and no mastery in him. As we have all been told, in this world a man must be either anvil or hammer, and it always seemed as if Pattison deliberately chose to be anvil—not merely in the shape of a renunciation of the delusive pomps and vanities of life, but in the truly questionable sense of doubting both whether he could do anything, and whether he even owed anything to the world in which he found himself.

The earliest launch was a disappointment. He had set his heart upon a first class, but he had not gone to work in the right way. Instead of concentrating his attention on the task in hand, he could only in later days look back with amazement 'at the fatuity of his arrangements and the snail-like progress with which he seemed to be satisfied.' He was content if, on his final review of Thucydides, he got through twenty or thirty chapters a day, and he reread Sophocles 'at the lazy rate of a hundred and fifty lines a day, instead of going over the difficult places only, which might have been done in a week. 'There must,' he says, 'have been idleness to boot, but it is difficult to draw the line between idleness and dawdling over work. I dawdled from a mixture of mental infirmity, bad habit, and the necessity of thoroughness if I was to understand, and not merely remember.' The dangerous delights of literary dispersion and dissipation attracted him. Among his books of recreation was Johnson's *Lives of the Poets*. 'This I took in slowly, page by page, as if by an instinct; but here was a congenial subject, to which, when free, I would return, and where I would set up my habitation.'

It was probably a reminiscence of these vacations at Hauxwell that inspired the beautiful passage in his *Milton*, where he contrasts the frosty *Ode to the Nativity* with the *Allegro and Penseroso*. 'The two idylls,' he says, 'breathe the free air of spring and summer and of the fields round Horton. They are thoroughly naturalistic; the choicest expression our language has yet found of the fresh charm of country life, not as that life is lived by the peasant, but as it is felt by a young and lettered student, issuing at early dawn or at sunset from his chamber and his books. All such sights and sounds and smells are here blended in that ineffable combination which once or twice, perhaps, in our lives has saluted our young senses before their perceptions were blunted by alcohol, by lust, or ambition, or diluted by the social distractions of great cities' (Pattison's *Milton*, 24).

For the examination school no preparation could have been worse. It was no wonder that so uncalculating an adjustment of means and ends resulted in a second class (1836). The class was not merely a misfortune in itself, but threatened to be a bar to the fulfilment of his lifelong dream of a fellowship. He tried his fortunes at University, where he was beaten by Faber; and at Oriel, his own college, where he was beaten by the present Dean of St. Paul's. 'There was such a moral beauty about Church,' it was said by a man not peculiarly sensitive about moral beauty, 'that they could not help liking him.' Though Pattison had failed, Newman sent him word that there were some who thought that he had done the best. He made two more unsuccessful attempts, in one of them the triumphant competitor being Stanley, the famous Dean of a later day. At last, in November 1838, he was elected to a Yorkshire fellowship at Lincoln College. 'No moment in all my life,' he says, 'has ever been so sweet as that Friday morning, when Radford's servant came in to announce my election, and to claim his five shillings for doing so.' Yet if the curtain of fate could have been raised, his election to the Lincoln fellowship might have disclosed itself as the central misfortune of his life.

'All this while,' he says, 'I was rushing into the whirlpool of Tractarianism; was very much noticed by Newman—in fact fanaticism was laying its deadly grip around me.' He had come up from Yorkshire with what he calls his 'home Puritan religion almost narrowed to two points—fear of God's wrath and faith in the doctrine of the Atonement.' He found Newman and his allies actively dissolving this hard creed by means of historical, philosophical, and religious elements which they summed up in the idea of the Church. This idea of the Church, as Pattison truly says, and as men so far removed from sympathy with dogma as J. S. Mill always admitted, 'was a widening of the horizon.' In another place (*Mind,* i. 83-88) the Rector shows the stages of speculation in Oxford during the present century. From 1800 or 1810 to 1830 the break-up of the old lethargy took the form of a vague intellectualism; free movement, but blind groping out of the mists of insular prejudice in which reaction against the French Revolution had wrapped us. Then came the second period from 1830 to 1845. Tractarianism was primarily a religious movement; it was a revival of the Church spirit which had been dormant since the expiry of Jacobitism at the accession of George III. But it rested on a conception, however imperfect, of universal history; and it even sought a basis for belief in a philosophic exposition of the principle of authority.

Pattison, like most of the superior minds then at Oxford, was not only attracted, but thoroughly overmastered by this great tide of thought. He worked at the Lives of the Saints, paid a visit to the cloisters at Littlemore, and was one of Newman's closest disciples, though he thinks it possible that Newman even then, with that curious instinct which so often marks the religious soul, had a scent of his latent rationalism. A female cousin, who eventually went over to Rome, counted for something among the influences that drove him into 'frantic Puseyism.' When the great secession came in 1845 Pattison somehow held back and was saved for a further development. Though he appeared to all intents and purposes as much of a Catholic at heart as Newman or any of them, it was probably his constitutional incapacity for heroic and decisive courses that made him, according to the Oxford legend, miss the omnibus. The first notion of the Church had expanded itself beyond the limits of the Anglican Communion, and been transformed into the wider idea of the Catholic Church. This in time underwent a further expansion.

> Now the idea of the Catholic Church is only a mode of
> conceiving the dealings of divine Providence with the whole
> race of mankind. Reflection on the history and condition

of humanity, taken as a whole, gradually convinced me that this theory of the relation of all living beings to the Supreme Being was too narrow and inadequate. It makes an equal Providence, the Father of all, care only for a mere handful of species, leaving the rest (such is the theory) to the chances of eternal misery. If God interferes at all to procure the happiness of mankind, it must be on a far more comprehensive scale than by providing for them a Church of which far the majority of them will never hear. It was on this line of thought, the details of which I need not pursue, that I passed out of the Catholic phase, but slowly, and in many years, to that highest development when all religions appear in their historical light as efforts of the human spirit to come to an understanding with that Unseen Power whose pressure it feels, but whose motives are a riddle. Thus Catholicism dropped off me as another husk which I had outgrown.

So a marked epoch came to its close, and this was one of the many forms in which the great Anglican impulse expended itself. While Newman and others sank their own individuality in religious devotion to authority and tradition, Pusey turned what had been discussion into controversy, and from a theologian became a powerful ecclesiastical manager. Others dropped their religious interests, and cultivated cynicism and letters. The railway mania, the political outbursts of 1848, utilitarian liberalism, all in turn swept over the Oxford field, and obliterated the old sanctuaries. Pattison went his own way alone. The time came when he looked back upon religion with some of the angry contempt with which George Eliot makes Bardo, the blind old humanist of the fifteenth century, speak of his son, who had left learning and liberal pursuits, 'that he might lash himself and howl at midnight with besotted friars—that he might go wandering on pilgrimages befitting men who knew no past older than the missal and the crucifix.'

It is a critical moment in life when middle age awakens a man from the illusions that have been crowning the earlier years with inward glory. Some are contemptuously willing to let the vision and the dream pass into easy oblivion, while they hasten to make up for lost time in close pursuit of the main chance. Others can forgive anything sooner than their own exploded ideal, and the ghost of their dead enthusiasm haunts them with an embittering presence. Pattison drops a good many expressions about his Anglo-Catholic days that betray something like vindictiveness—which is certainly not philosophical, whatever else it was. But his intellectual faculties were too strong to let him feed on the poison of a reactionary antipathy to a deserted faith. Puseyism, as he says, dropped away from him for lack of nutrition of the religious brain,—which perhaps at the best was more like an artificial limb than a natural organ in a man of Pattison's constitution. For some five years he was inspired by a new and more genuine enthusiasm—for forming and influencing the minds of the young. He found that he was the possessor of what, for lack of a better name, he calls a magnetic power in dealing with the students, and his moral ascendency enabled him to make Lincoln the best managed college in Oxford.

From 1848 to 1851 he describes his absorption in the work of the college as complete. It excluded all other thoughts. In November that incident occurred which he calls the catastrophe of his life. The headship of the college fell vacant, and for several weeks he was led to believe that this valuable prize was within his grasp. At first the invincible diffidence of his nature made it hard for him to realise that exaltation so splendid was possible. But the prospect once opened, fastened with a fatally violent hold upon his imagination. The fellows of Lincoln College, who were the electors, were at that time a terribly degraded body. The majority of them were no more capable of caring for literature, knowledge, education, books, or learning than Squire Western or Commodore Trunnion. One of them, says Pattison, had been reduced by thirty years of the Lincoln common-room to a torpor almost childish. Another was 'a wretched *crétin* of the name of Gibbs, who was always glad to come and booze at the college port a week or two when his vote was wanted in support of college abuses.' The description of a third, who still survives, is veiled by editorial charity behind significant asterisks. That Pattison should be popular with such a gang was impossible. Such an Alceste was a standing nuisance and reproach to the rustic Acastes and Clitandres of the Lincoln bursary. They might have tolerated his intellect and overlooked his industry, if his intellect and his industry had not spoiled his sociability. But irony and the *ars tacendi* are not favourite ingredients in the boon companion. Pattison never stayed in the common-room later than eight in the evening, and a man was no better than a skeleton at a feast who left good fellows for the sake of going over an essay with a pupil, instead of taking a hand at whist or helping them through another bottle.

We need not follow the details of the story. Pattison has told them over again, with a minuteness and a sourness that show how the shabby business rankled in his soul to the very last. It was no battle of giants, like the immortal Thirty Years' War between Bentley and the Fellows of Trinity. The election at Lincoln College, which was a scandal in the university for many a long day after, was simply a tissue of paltry machinations, in which weakness, cunning, spite, and a fair spice of downright lying showed that a learned society, even of clergymen, may seethe and boil with the passions of the very refuse of humanity. Intricate and unclean intrigues ended, by a curious turn of the wheel, in the election of a grotesque divine, whom Pattison, with an energy of phrase that recalls the amenities of ecclesiastical controversy in the sixteenth century, roundly designates in so many words as a satyr, a ruffian, and a wild beast. The poor man was certainly illiterate and boorish to a degree that was a standing marvel to all ingenuous youths who came up to Lincoln College between 1850 and 1860. His manners, bearing, and accomplishments were more fitted for the porter of a workhouse than for the head of a college. But he served the turn by keeping out Pattison's rival, and whatever discredit he brought upon the society must be shared by those who, with Pattison at their head, brought him in against a better man. All this unsavoury story might as well have been left where it was.

The reaction was incredibly severe. There has been nothing equal to it since the days of the Psalmist were consumed like smoke, and his heart was withered like grass. 'My mental forces,' says Pattison, 'were paralysed by the shock; a blank, dumb despair filled me; a chronic heartache took possession of me, perceptible even through sleep. As consciousness gradually returned in the morning, it was only to bring with it a livelier sense of the cruelty of the situation into which I had been brought.' He lay in bed until ten o'clock every morning to prolong the semi-oblivion of sleep. Work was impossible. If he read, it was without any object beyond semi-forgetfulness. He was too much benumbed and stupefied to calculate the future. He went through the forms of lecturing, but the life and spirit were gone. Teaching became as odious to him as it had once been delightful. His Satan, as he calls the most active of the enemies who had thus ruined his paradise, planned new operations against him, by trying, on the grounds of some neglected formality, to oust him from his fellowship. 'Here,' cries Pattison, 'was a new abyss opened beneath my feet! My bare livelihood, for I had nothing except my fellowship to live upon, was threatened; it seemed not unlikely that I should be turned into the streets to starve. Visitatorial law, what it might contain! It loomed before me like an Indian jungle, out of which might issue venomous reptiles, man-eating tigers, for my destruction.'

This is not the language of half-humorous exaggeration, but a literal account of a mind as much overthrown from its true balance as is disclosed in the most morbid page of Rousseau's *Confessions*. For months and months after the burden of 'dull, insensible wretchedness,' 'bitter heartache,' weighed upon him with unabated oppression. More than a year after the catastrophe the sombre entries still figure in his diary:—'Very weary and wretched both yesterday and to-day: all the savour of life is departed:'— 'Very wretched all yesterday and to-day: dull, gloomy, blank; sleep itself is turned to sorrow.' Nearly two whole years after the same clouds still blacken the sky. 'I have nothing to which I look forward with any satisfaction: no prospects; my life seems to have come to an end, my strength gone, my energies paralysed, and all my hopes dispersed.'

It is true that frustrated ambition was not the only key to this frightfully abject abasement. We may readily believe him when he says that the personal disappointment was a minor ingredient in the total of mental suffering that he was now undergoing. His whole heart and pride had in the last few years been invested in the success of the college; it was the thing on which he had set all his affections; in a fortnight the foundation of his work was broken up; and the wretched and deteriorated condition of the undergraduates became as poison in his daily cup. That may all be true enough. Still, whatever elements of a generous public spirit sharply baffled may have entered into this extraordinary moral breakdown, it must be pronounced a painfully unmanly and unedifying exhibition. It says a great deal for the Rector's honesty and sincerity in these pages, that he should not have shrunk from giving so faithful and prominent an account of a weakness and a self-abandonment which he knew well enough that the world will only excuse in two circumstances. The world forgives almost anything to a man in the crisis of a sore spiritual wrestle for faith and vision and an Everlasting Yea; and almost anything to one prostrated by the shock of an irreparable personal bereavement. But that anybody with character of common healthiness should founder and make shipwreck of his life because two or three unclean creatures had played him a trick after their kind, is as incredible as that a three-decker should go down in a street puddle.

It will not do to say that lack of fortitude is a mark of the man of letters. To measure Pattison's astounding collapse, we have a right to recall Johnson, Scott, Carlyle, and a host of smaller men, whom no vexations, chagrins, and perversities of fate could daunt from fighting the battle out. Pattison was thirty-eight when he missed the headship of his college. Diderot was about the same age when the torments against which he had struggled for the best part of twenty arduous years in his gigantic task seemed to reach the very climax of distraction. 'My dear master,' he wrote to Voltaire, in words which it is a refreshment under the circumstances to recall and to transcribe, 'my dear master, I am over forty. I am tired out with tricks and shufflings. I cry from morning till night for rest, rest; and scarcely a day passes when I am not tempted to go and live in obscurity and die in peace in the depths of my old country. Be useful to men! Is it certain that one does more than amuse them, and that there is much difference between the philosopher and the flute-player? They listen to one and the other with pleasure or with disdain, and they remain just what they were. But there is more spleen than sense in all this, I know—and back I go to the Encyclopædia.' And back he went—that is the great point—with courage unabated and indomitable, labouring with sword in one hand and trowel in the other, until he had set the last stone on his enormous fabric.

Several years went by before Pattison's mind recovered spring and equilibrium, and the unstrung nerves were restored to energy. Fishing, the open air, solitude, scenery, slowly repaired the moral ravages of the college election. The fly rod 'was precisely the resource of which my wounded nature stood in need.' About the middle of April, after long and anxious preparation of rods and tackle, with a box of books and a store of tobacco, he used to set out for the north. He fished the streams of Uredale and Swaledale; thence he pushed on to the Eden and the waters of the Border, to Perthshire, to Loch Maree, Gairloch, Skye, and the far north. When September came, he set off for rambles in Germany. He travelled on foot, delighting in the discovery of nooks and corners that were not mentioned in the guidebooks. Then he would return to his rooms in college, and live among his books. To the undergraduates of that day he was a solemn and mysterious figure. He spoke to no one, saluted no one, and kept his eyes steadily fixed on infinite space. He dined at the high table, but uttered no word. He never played the part of host, nor did he ever seem to be a guest. He read the service in chapel when his turn came: his voice had a creaking and impassive tone, and his pace was too deliberate to please young men with a morning appetite. As he says here, he was a complete stranger in the college. We looked upon him with the awe proper to one who was supposed to combine boundless erudition with an impenetrable misanthropy. In reading the fourth book of the Ethics, we regarded the description of the High-souled Man, with his slow movements, his deep tones, his deliberate speech, his irony, his contempt for human things, and all the rest of the paraphernalia of that most singular personage, as the model of the inscrutable sage in the rooms under the clock. Pattison was understood to be the Megalopsuchos in the flesh. It would have been better for him if he could have realised the truth of the healthy maxim that nobody is ever either so happy or so unhappy as he thinks. He would have been wiser if he could have seen the force in the monition of Goethe:—

> Willst du dir ein hübsch Leben zimmern,
> Must ums Vergangne dich nicht bekümmern,
> Und wäre dir auch was verloren,
> Musst immer thun wie neu geboren;
> Was jeder Tag will, sollst du fragen,
> Was jeder Tag will, wird er sagen;
> Musst dich an eignem Thun ergetzen,
> Was andre thun, das wirst du schätzen;
> Besonders keinen Menschen hassen,
> Und das Uebrige Gott überlassen.

(*Zahme Xenien*, iv.)

> *Wouldst fashion for thyself a seemly life?—*
> *Then fret not over what is past and gone;*
> *And spite of all thou mayst have lost behind*
> *Yet act as if thy life were just begun:*
> *What each day wills, enough for thee to know,*
> *What each day wills, the day itself will tell;*

Do thine own task, and be therewith content,
What others do, that shalt thou fairly judge;
Be sure that thou no brother mortal hate.
And all besides leave to the master Power.

At length 'the years of defeat and despair,' as he calls them, came to an end, though 'the mental and moral deterioration' that belonged to them left heavy traces to the very close of his life. He took a lively interest in the discussions that were stirred by the famous University Commission, and contributed ideas to the subject of academic reform on more sides than one. But such matters he found desultory and unsatisfying; he was in a state of famine; his mind was suffering, not growing; he was becoming brooding, melancholy, taciturn, and finally pessimist. Pattison was five-and-forty before he reached the conception of what became his final ideal, as it had been in a slightly different shape his first and earliest. He had always been a voracious reader. When 'the flood of the Tractarian infatuation broke over him, he naturally concentrated his studies on the Fathers and on Church History. That phase, in his own term, took eight years out of his life. Then for five years more he was absorbed in teaching and forming the young mind. The catastrophe came, and for five or six years after that he still remained far below 'the pure and unselfish conception of the life of the true student, which dawned upon him afterwards, and which Goethe, it seems, already possessed at thirty.' Up to this time—the year 1857, or a little later—his aims and thoughts had been, in his own violent phrase, polluted and disfigured by literary ambition. He had felt the desire to be before the world as a writer, and had hitherto shared 'the vulgar fallacy that a literary life meant a life devoted to the making of books.' 'It cost me years more of extrication of thought before I rose to *the conception that the highest life is the art to live*, and that both men, women, and books are equally essential ingredients of such a life' .

We may notice in passing, what any one will see for himself, that in contrasting his new conception so triumphantly with the vulgar fallacy from which he had shaken himself free, the Rector went very near to begging the question. When Carlyle, in the strength of his reaction against morbid introspective Byronism, cried aloud to all men in their several vocation, '*Produce, produce; be it but the infinitesimallest product, produce,*' he meant to include production as an element inside the art of living, and an indispensable part and parcel of it. The making of books may or may not belong to the art of living. It depends upon the faculty and gift of the individual. It would have been more philosophical if, instead of ranking the life of study for its own sake above the life of composition and the preparation for composition, Pattison had been content with saying that some men have the impulse towards literary production, while in others the impulse is strongest for acquisition, and that he found out one day that nature had placed him in the latter and rarer class. It is no case of ethical or intellectual superiority, as he fondly supposed, but only diversity of gift.

We must turn to the volume on Casaubon for a fuller interpretation of the oracle. 'The scholar,' says the author, 'is greater than his books. The result of his labours is not so many thousand pages in folio, but himself.... Learning is a peculiar compound of memory, imagination, scientific habit, accurate observation, all concentrated, through a prolonged period, on the analysis of the remains of literature. The result of this sustained mental endeavour is not a book, but a man. It cannot be embodied in print, it consists in the living word. True learning does not consist in the possession of a stock of facts—the merit of a dictionary—but in the discerning spirit, a power of appreciation, *judicium* as it was called in the sixteenth century— which is the result of the possession of a stock of facts.'

The great object, then, is to bring the mind into such a condition of training and cultivation that it shall be a perfect mirror of past times, and of the present, so far as the incompleteness of the present will permit, 'in true outline and proportion.' Mommsen, Grote, Droysen, fall short of the ideal, because they drugged ancient history with modern politics. The Jesuit learning of the sixteenth century was sham learning, because it was tainted with the interested motives of Church patriotism. To search antiquity with polemical objects in view, is destructive of 'that equilibrium of the reason, the imagination, and the taste, that even temper of philosophical calm, that singleness of purpose,' which were all required for Pattison's ideal scholar. The active man has his uses, he sometimes, but never very cheerfully, admits. Those who at the opening of the seventeenth century fought in literature, in the council-chamber, in the field, against the Church revival of their day, may be counted among worthies and benefactors. 'But for all this, it remains true, that in the intellectual sphere grasp and mastery are incompatible with the exigencies of a struggle.'

The reader will hardly retain gravity of feature before the self-indulgent, self-deceiving sophistication of a canon, which actually excludes from grasp and mastery in the intellectual sphere Dante, Milton, and Burke. Pattison repeats in his closing pages his lamentable refrain that the author of *Paradise Lost* should have forsaken poetry for more than twenty years 'for a noisy pamphlet brawl, and the unworthy drudgery of Secretary to the Council Board' . He had said the same thing in twenty places in his book on Milton. He transcribes unmoved the great poet's account of his own state of mind, after the physicians had warned him that if he persisted in using his remaining eye for his pamphlet, he would lose that too. 'The choice lay before me,' says Milton, 'between dereliction of a supreme duty and loss of eyesight: in such a case I could not listen to the physician, not if Æsculapius himself had spoken from his sanctuary. I could not but obey that inward monitor, I knew not what, that spake to me from heaven. I considered with myself that many had purchased less good with worse ill, as they who give their lives to reap only glory, and I therefore concluded to employ the little remaining eyesight I was to enjoy in doing this, the greatest service to the common weal it was in my power to render.' And so he wrote the *Second Defence*, and yet lived long enough, and preserved sublimity of imagination enough, to write the *Paradise Lost* as well. Mr. Goldwin Smith goes nearer the mark than the Rector when he insists that 'the tension and elevation which Milton's nature had undergone in the mighty struggle, together with the heroic dedication of his faculties to the most serious objects, must have had not a little to do both with the final choice of his subject and with the tone of his poem. "The great Puritan epic" could hardly have been written by any one but a militant Puritan' (*Lectures and Essays*, p. 324). In the last page of his *Memoirs*, Pattison taxes the poet with being carried away by the aims of 'a party whose aims he idealised.' As if the highest fruitfulness of intellect were ever reached without this generous faculty of idealisation, which Pattison, here and always, viewed with such icy coldness. Napoleon used to say that what was most fatal to a general was a knack of combining objects into pictures. A good officer, he said, never makes pictures; he sees objects, as through a field-glass, exactly as they are. In the art of war let us take Napoleon's word for this; but in 'the art to live' a man who dreads to idealise aims or to make pictures, who can think of nothing finer than being what Aristotle calls αυθέκαστος, or taking everything literally for what it is, will sooner or later find his faculties benumbed and his work narrowed to something for which nobody but himself will care, and for which he will not himself always care with any sincerity or depth of interest.

Let us take another illustration of the false exclusiveness of the definition, in which Pattison erected a peculiar constitutional idiosyncrasy into a complete and final law for the life literary. He used to contend that in many respects the most admirable literary figure of the eighteenth century was the poet Gray. Gray, he would say, never thought that devotion to letters meant the making of books. He gave himself up for the most part to ceaseless observation and acquisition. By travelling, reading, noting, with a patient industry that would not allow itself to be diverted or perturbed, he sought and gained the discerning spirit and the power of appreciation which make not a book but a man. He annotated the volumes that he read with judgment; he kept botanical calendars and thermometrical registers; he had a lively curiosity all round; and, in Gray's own words, he deemed it a sufficient object of his studies to know, wherever he was, what lay within reach that was worth seeing—whether building, ruin, park, garden, prospect, picture, or monument—to whom it had ever belonged, and what had been the characteristic and taste of different ages. 'Turn author,' said Gray, 'and straightway you expose yourself to pit, boxes, and gallery: any coxcomb in the world may come in and hiss if he pleases; ay, and what is almost as bad, clap too, and you cannot hinder him.'

Nobody will be inclined to quarrel with Gray's way of passing his life, and the poet who had produced so exquisite a masterpiece as the Elegy had a fair right to spend the rest of his days as he pleased. But the temptations to confound a finicking dilettantism with the 'art to live' are so strong, that it is worth while to correct the Rector's admiration for Gray by looking on another picture—one of Gray's most famous contemporaries, who in variety of interest and breadth of acquired knowledge was certainly not inferior to him, but enormously his superior. Lessing died when he was fifty-two (1729-1781); his life was two years shorter than Gray's (1716-1771), and nearly twenty years shorter than Pattison's (1813-1884). The Rector would have been the last man to deny that the author of *Laoköon* and the *Wolfenbüttel Fragments* abounded in the discerning spirit and the power of appreciation. Yet Lessing was one of the most incessantly productive minds of his age. In art, in religion, in literature, in the drama, in the whole field of criticism, he launched ideas of sovereign importance, both for his own and following times, and, in *Nathan the Wise*, the truest and best mind of the eighteenth century found its gravest and noblest voice. Well might George Eliot at the Berlin theatre feel her heart swelling and the tears coming into her eyes as she 'listened to the noble words of dear Lessing, whose great spirit lives immortally in this crowning work of his' (*Life*, i. 364). Yet so far were 'grasp and mastery' from being incompatible with the exigencies of a struggle, that the varied, supple, and splendid powers of Lessing were exercised from first to last in an atmosphere of controversy. Instead of delicately nursing the theoretic life in the luxury of the academic cloister, he was forced to work like a slave upon the most uncongenial tasks for a very modest share of daily bread. 'I only wished to have things like other men,' he said in a phrase of pathetic simplicity, at the end of his few short months of wedded happiness; 'I have had but sorry success.' Harassed by small persecutions, beset by paltry debts, passing months in loneliness and in indigence, he was yet so possessed, not indeed by the winged dæmon of poetic creation, but by the irrepressible impulse and energy of production, that the power of his intellect triumphed over every obstacle, and made him one of the greatest forces in the wide history of European literature. Our whole heart goes out to a man who thus, in spite alike of his own impetuous stumbles and the blind buffets of unrelenting fate, yet persevered to the last in laborious, honest, spontaneous, and almost artless fidelity to the use of his talent, and after each repulse only came on the more eagerly to 'live and act and serve the future hours.' It was Lessing and not Rousseau whom Carlyle ought to have taken for his type of the Hero as Man of Letters.

The present writer will not be suspected of the presumption of hinting or implying that Pattison himself was a *dilettante,* or anything like one. There never was a more impertinent blunder than when people professed to identify the shrewdest and most widely competent critic of his day with the Mr. Casaubon of the novel, and his absurd Key to all Mythologies. The Rector's standard of equipment was the highest of our time. 'A critic's education,' he said, 'is not complete till he has in his mind a conception of the successive phases of thought and feeling from the beginning of letters. Though he need not read every book, he must have surveyed literature in its totality. Partial knowledge of literature is no knowledge' (*Fortnightly Review*, Nov. 1877, p. 670). For a man to know his way about in the world of printed books, to find the key to knowledge, to learn the map of literature, 'requires a long apprenticeship. This is a point few men can hope to reach much before the age of forty' (*Milton*, 110).

There was no dilettantism here. And one must say much more than that. Many of those in whom the love of knowledge is liveliest omit from their curiosity that part of knowledge which is, to say the least of it, as interesting as all the rest—insight, namely, into the motives, character, conduct, doctrines, fortunes of the individual man. It was not so with Pattison. He was essentially a bookman, but of that high type—the only type that is worthy of a spark of our admiration—which explores through books the voyages of the human reason, the shifting impulses of the human heart, the chequered fortunes of great human conceptions. Pattison knew that he is very poorly equipped for the art of criticism who has not trained himself in the observant analysis of character, and has not realised that the writer who seeks to give richness, body, and flavour to his work must not linger exclusively among texts or abstract ideas or general movements or literary effects, but must tell us something about the moral and intellectual configuration of those with whom he deals. I had transcribed, for an example, his account of Erasmus, but the article is growing long, and the reader may find it for himself in the *Encyclopædia Britannica* (viii. 515 *a*).

Though nobody was ever much less of a man of the world in one sense, yet Pattison's mind was always in the world. In company he often looked as if he were thinking of the futility of dinner-party dialectics, where all goes too fast for truth, where people miss one another's points and their own, where nobody convinces or is convinced, and where there is much surface excitement with little real stimulation. That so shrewd a man should have seen so obvious a fact as all this was certain. But he knew that the world is the real thing, that the proper study of mankind is man, and that if books must be counted more instructive and nourishing than affairs, as he thought them to be, it is still only because they are the most complete record of what is permanent, elevated, and eternal in the mind and act of man. Study with him did not mean the compilation of careful abstracts of books, nor did it even mean the historic filiation of thoughts and beliefs. It was the building up before the mind's eye of definite conceptions as to what manner of men had been bred by the diversified agencies of human history, and how given thoughts had shaped the progress of the race. This is what, among other things, led him to spend so much time on the circle of Pope and Addison and Swift.

We have let fall a phrase about the progress of the race, but it hardly had a place in Pattison's own vocabulary. 'While the advances,' he said, 'made by objective science and its industrial applications are palpable and undeniable everywhere around us, it is a matter of doubt and dispute if our social and moral advance towards happiness and virtue has been great or any.' The selfishness of mankind might seem to be a constant quantity, neither much abated nor much increased since history began. Italy and France are in most material points not more civilised than they were in the second century of our era. The reign of law and justice has no doubt extended into the reign of hyperborean ice and over Sarmatian plains: but then Spain, has relapsed into a double barbarism by engrafting Catholic superstition upon Iberian ferocity. If we look Eastward, we see a horde of barbarians in occupation of the garden of the Old World, not as settlers, but as destroyers (*Age of Reason*, in *Fortnightly Review*, March 1877, 357-361).

The same prepossessions led him to think that all the true things had been said, and one could do no better than hunt them up again for new uses. Our business was, like Old Mortality, to clear out and cut afresh inscriptions that had been made illegible by time and storm. At least this delivered him from the senseless vanity of originality and personal appropriation. We feel sure that if he found that a thought which he had believed to be new had been expressed in literature before, he would have been pleased and not mortified. No reflection of his own could give him half as much satisfaction as an apt citation from some one else. He once complained of the writer of the article on Comte in the *Encyclopædia* for speaking with too much deference as to Comte's personality. 'That overweening French vanity and egotism not only overshadows great gifts, but impoverishes the character which nourished such a sentiment. It is not one of the weaknesses which we overlook in great men, and which are to go for nothing.' Of overweening egotism Pattison himself at any rate had none. This was partly due to his theory of history, and partly, too, no doubt, to his inborn discouragement of spirit. He always professed to be greatly relieved when an editor assured him that his work was of the quality that might have been expected from him. 'Having lived to be sixty-three,' he wrote on one of these occasions, 'without finding out why the public embrace or reject what is written for their benefit, I presume I shall now never make the discovery.' And this was perfectly sincere.

The first draft of his *Life of Milton* was found to exceed the utmost limits of what was possible by some thirty or forty pages. Without a single movement of importunity or complaint he cut off the excess, though it amounted to a considerable fraction of what he had done. 'In any case,' he said, 'it is all on Milton; there is no digression on public affairs, and much which might have gone in with advantage to the completeness of the story has been entirely passed over, *e.g.* history of his posthumous fame, Bentley's emendations, *et cetera*.' It almost seemed as if he had a private satisfaction in a literary mishap of this kind: it was an unexpected corroboration of his standing conclusion that this is the most stupid and perverse of all possible worlds.

'My one scheme,' he wrote to a friend in 1877, 'that of a history of the eighteenth century, having been forestalled by Leslie Stephen, and the collections, of years having been rendered useless, I am entirely out of gear, and cannot settle to anything.' His correspondent urged the Rector to consider and reconsider. It would be one of the most deplorable misfortunes in literature if he were thus to waste the mature fruit of the study of a lifetime. It was as unreasonable as if Raphael or Titian had refused to paint a Madonna simply because other people had painted Madonnas before them. Some subjects, no doubt, were treated once for all; if Southey had written his history of the Peninsular war after Napier, he would have done a silly thing, and his book would have been damned unread. But what reason was there why we should not have half a dozen books on English thought in the eighteenth century? Would not Grote have inflicted a heavy loss upon us if he had been frightened out of his plan by Thirlwall? And so forth, and so forth. But all such importunities were of no avail. 'I have pondered over your letter,' Pattison replied, 'but without being able to arrive at any resolution of any kind.' Of course one knew that in effect temperament had already cast the resolution for him in letters of iron before our eyes.

We are not aware whether any considerable work has been left behind. His first great scheme, as he tells us here , was a history of learning from the Renaissance. Then he contracted his views to a history of the French school of Philology, beginning with Budæus and the Delphin classics. Finally, his ambition was narrowed to fragments. The book on *Isaac Casaubon*, published ten years ago, is a definite and valuable literary product. But the great work would have been the vindication of Scaliger, for which he had been getting materials together for thirty years. Many portions, he says, were already written out in their definite form, and twelve months would have completed it. Alas, a man should not go on trusting until his seventieth year that there is still plenty of daylight. He contributed five biographies to the new edition of the *Encyclopædia Britannica*. The articles on Bentley, Erasmus, Grotius, More, and Macaulay are from his pen. They are all terse, luminous, and finished, and the only complaint that one can make against them is that our instructor parts company from us too soon. It is a stroke of literary humour after Pattison's own heart that Bentley, the mightiest of English scholars, should fill no more space in the Encyclopædic pantheon than Alford, who was hardly even the mightiest of English deans. But the fault was more probably with the rector's parsimony of words than with the editor. In 1877 he delivered a lecture, afterwards reprinted in one of the reviews, on Books and Critics. It is not without the usual piquancy and the usual cynicism, but he had nothing particular to say, except to tell his audience that a small house is no excuse for absence of books, inasmuch as a set of shelves, thirteen feet by ten, and six inches deep, will accommodate nearly a thousand octavos; and to hint that a man making a thousand a year, who spends less than a pound a week on books, ought to be ashamed of himself. There are some other fugitive pieces scattered in the periodicals of the day. In 1871 and 1872 he published editions of the *Essay on Man* and *The Satires and Epistles* of Pope. Ten years before that he had been at last elected to the headship of his college, but the old enthusiasm for influencing young minds was dead. We have spoken of the Rector's timidity and impotence in practical things. Yet it is fair to remember the persevering courage with which he pleaded one unpopular cause. As Mr. Morison said not long ago, his writings on university organisation, the most important of which appeared in 1868, are a noble monument of patient zeal in the cause for which he cared most. 'Pattison never lost heart, never ceased holding up his ideal of what a university should be, viz. a metropolis of learning in which would be collected and grouped into their various faculties the best scholars and *savants* the country could produce, all working with generous emulation to increase the merit and renown of their chairs. If England ever does obtain such a university, it will be in no small measure to Pattison that she will owe it.'

Yet when the record is completed, it falls short of what might have been expected from one with so many natural endowments, such unrivalled opportunities, such undoubted sincerity of interest. Pattison had none of what so much delighted Carlyle in Ram-Dass, the Hindoo man-god. When asked what he meant to do for the sins of men, Ram-Dass at once made answer that he had fire enough in his belly to burn up all the sins of the world. Of this abdominal flame Pattison had not a spark. Nor had he that awful sense which no humanism could extinguish in Milton, of service as 'ever in the great Taskmaster's eye.' Nor had he, finally, that civil and secular enthusiasm which made men like Bentham and Mill into great workers and benefactors of their kind. Pattison was of the mind of Fra Paolo in a letter to Casaubon. 'As long as there are men there will be fanaticism. The wisest man has warned us not to expect the world ever to improve so much that the better part of mankind will be the majority. No wise man ever undertakes to correct the disorders of the public estate. He who cannot endure the madness of the public, but goeth about to think he can cure it, is himself no less mad than the rest. So, sing to yourself and the muses.' The muses never yet inspired with their highest tunes, whether in prose or verse, men of this degree of unfaith.

NOTES

* 9 7 8 9 3 6 0 4 6 7 4 1 8 *